Walter Foster
Jr.

learn to draw
Dinosaurs

Step-by-step instructions for more than 25 prehistoric creatures

ILLUSTRATED BY ROBBIN CUDDY

Brimming with creative inspiration, how-to projects, and useful information to enrich your everyday life, Quarto Knows is a favorite destination for those pursuing their interests and passions. Visit our site and dig deeper with our books into your area of interest: Quarto Creates, Quarto Cooks, Quarto Homes, Quarto Lives, Quarto Drives, Quarto Explores, Quarto Gifts, or Quarto Kids.

© 2015 Quarto Publishing Group USA Inc.
Photographs © Shutterstock, except photographs on pages 48 and 50 © Getty Images.

First published in 2015 by Walter Foster Jr., an imprint of The Quarto Group.
26391 Crown Valley Parkway, Suite 220, Mission Viejo, CA 92691, USA.
T (949) 380-7510 **F** (949) 380-7575 **www.QuartoKnows.com**

Walter Foster Jr. titles are also available at discount for retail, wholesale, promotional, and bulk purchase. For details, contact the Special Sales Manager by email at specialsales@quarto.com or by mail at The Quarto Group, Attn: Special Sales Manager, 100 Cummings Center, Suite 265D, Beverly, MA 01915, USA.

ISBN: 978-1-63322-030-0

Printed in China
19 18 17 16 15 14 13 12 11

Table of Contents

Tools & Materials

There's more than one way to bring dinosaurs to life on paper—you can use crayons, markers, colored pencils, or even paints. Just be sure you have plenty of good dino colors—browns, greens, and purples.

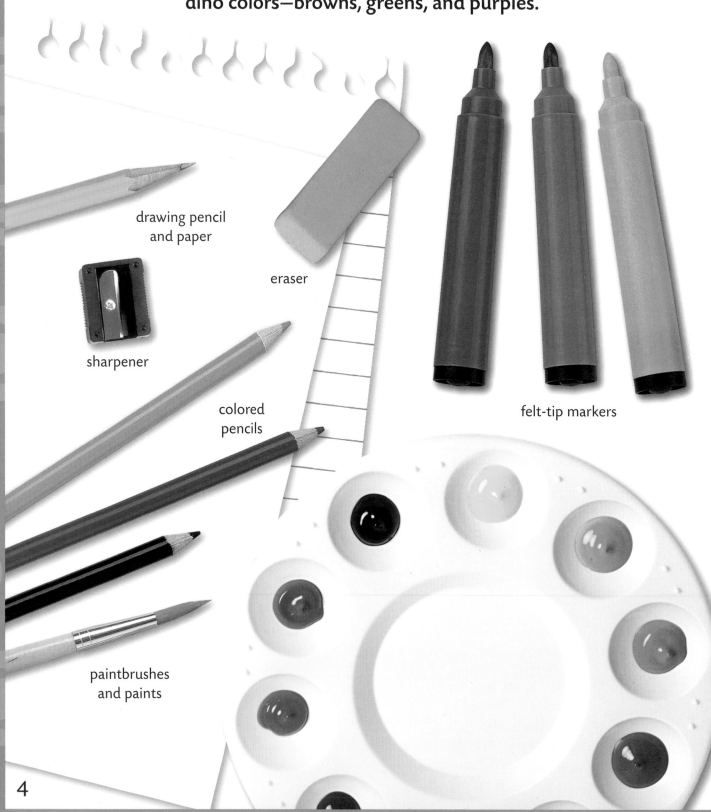

drawing pencil and paper

eraser

sharpener

colored pencils

felt-tip markers

paintbrushes and paints

How to Use This Book

The drawings in this book are made up of basic shapes, such as circles, triangles, and rectangles. Practice drawing the shapes below.

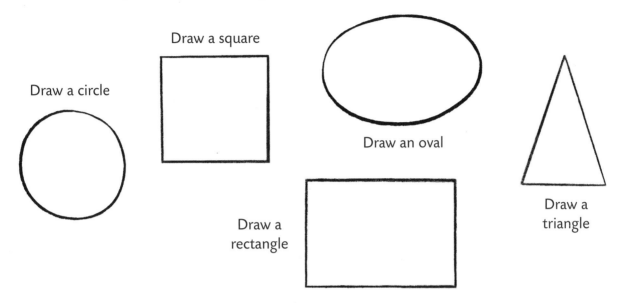

Draw a square

Draw a circle

Draw an oval

Draw a rectangle

Draw a triangle

Notice how these drawings begin with basic shapes.

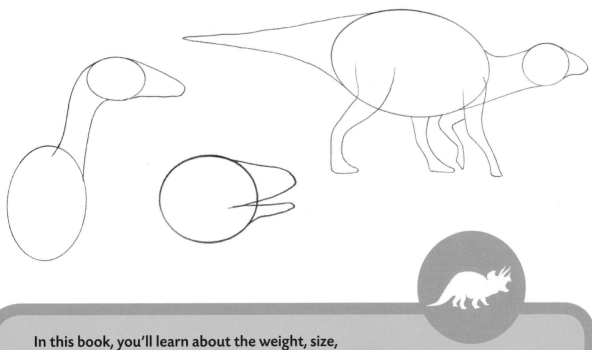

In this book, you'll learn about the weight, size, diet, and appearance of each featured prehistoric creature. Look for mini quizzes along the way to test your knowledge and learn exciting facts!

Look for this symbol, and check your answers on page 64!

It's Dinosaur Time!

Dinosaurs (which means "terrible lizards" in Ancient Greek) existed between 65 million and 245 million years ago during the Mesozoic Era, when the earth was much different than it is today. This era breaks down into three geological periods (or spans of time): the Cretaceous, Jurassic, and Triassic. Within each geological period, different groupings of dinosaurs existed.

Mesozoic Era
252 to 66 million years ago

Triassic Period
252 to 201 million years ago

Jurassic Period
201 to 145 million years ago

Cretaceous Period
145 to 65 million years ago

Dinosaurs existed on earth for about 180 million years—
an extraordinarily long time. Think about this: Modern man has
only been on earth for about 200,000 years!

Fun Fact!

About 250 million years ago, all of the continents were connected in one large, swampy land mass called "Pangaea." During the Triassic Period, the earth's tectonic plates slowly separated the land into continents, causing volcanic activity and climate change.

Dino Bites

Not all dinosaurs were meat-eating monsters! Some ate plants, some ate meat, and some ate both. Below are the terms used to describe dinosaurs based on their diets.

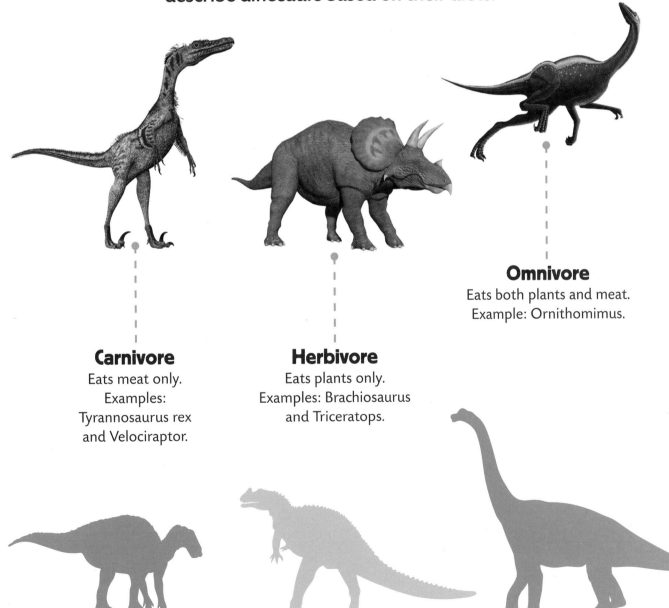

Omnivore
Eats both plants and meat.
Example: Ornithomimus.

Carnivore
Eats meat only.
Examples:
Tyrannosaurus rex
and Velociraptor.

Herbivore
Eats plants only.
Examples: Brachiosaurus
and Triceratops.

Ankylosaurus

Fun Fact!

Ankylosaurus means "fused lizard" in Ancient Greek, referring to the fused, knobby plates of armor that covered its body and protected it from enemies.

Diet:
Herbivore

Weight:
4 tons

Size:
33 feet long

This massive dinosaur had a square head and a beaked mouth. An outer layer of bony plates and a club-like tail offered protection from predators.

Did You Know?

Ankylosaurus roamed the forests of North America during the Cretaceous Period.

Pteranodon

Weight:
35 pounds

Diet:
Carnivore

Size: 20-foot
wingspan

Fun Fact!

Pteranodon is not technically a dinosaur. Instead, it's part of a group of animals called "pterosaurs," which were furry, flying reptiles that existed during the time of dinosaurs. These meat eaters were both hunters and scavengers.

Pteranodon was a flying creature of the Late Cretaceous that had large eyes, a sharp jaw, a pointed head crest, and a wingspan of more than 20 feet.

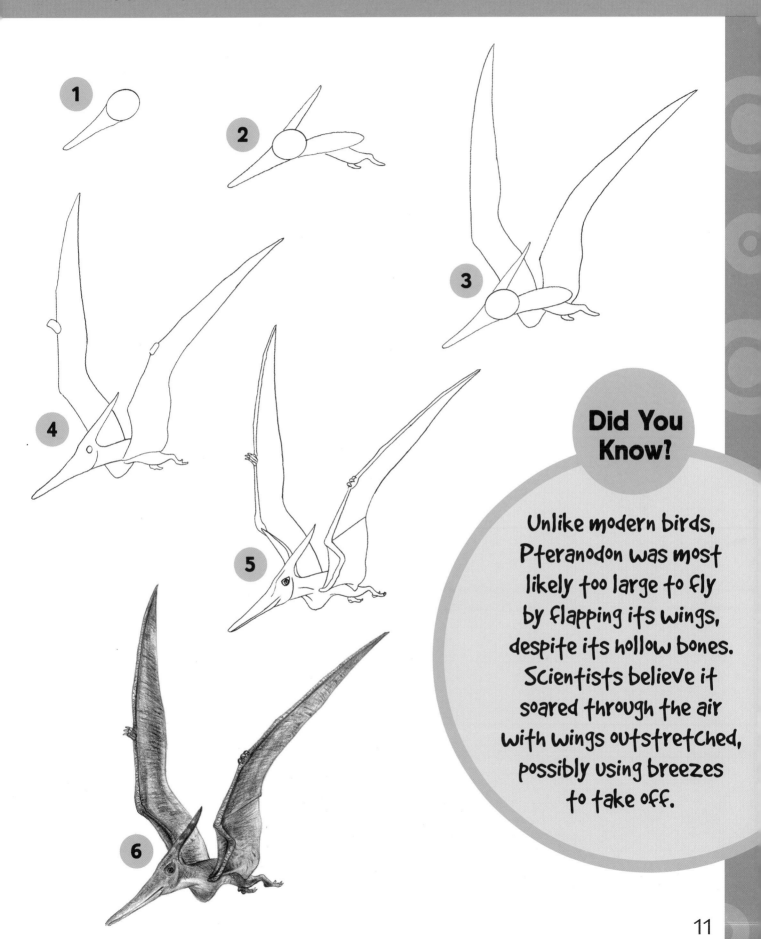

Did You Know?

Unlike modern birds, Pteranodon was most likely too large to fly by flapping its wings, despite its hollow bones. Scientists believe it soared through the air with wings outstretched, possibly using breezes to take off.

Dimetrodon

Nobody is certain about the function of the Dimetrodon's "sail." Some scientists suggest that it helped the creature control its body temperature, others suggest it served as camouflage, and still others believe it helped with mate selection.

Fun Fact!

Diet:
Carnivore

Size:
11.5 feet long

Weight:
500 pounds

This distinct lizard-like creature had a large head, powerful jaws, and short limbs. Long, vertical spines along its back created a humped "sail" or crest.

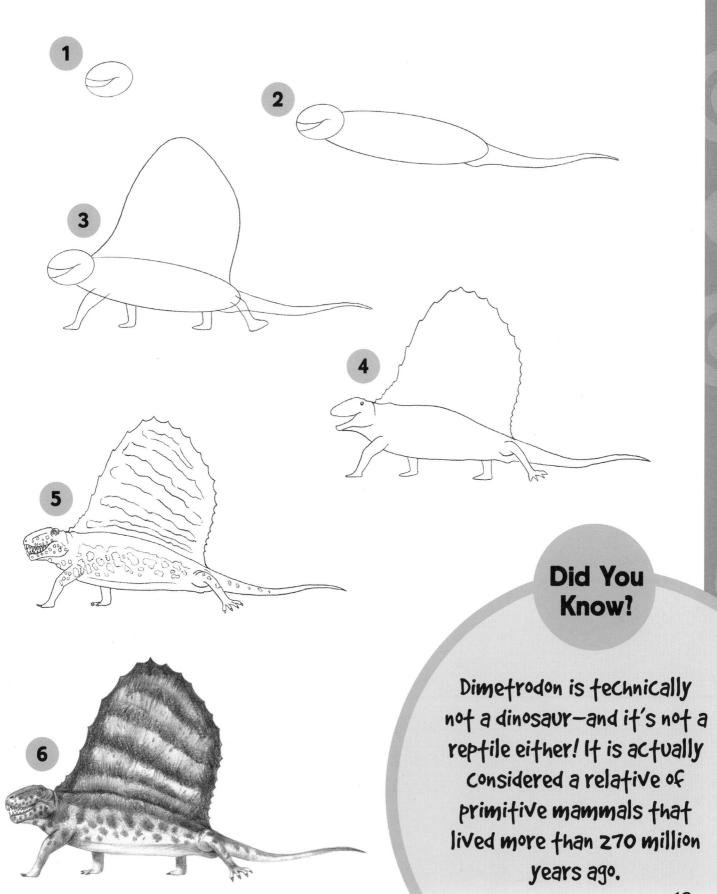

Did You Know?

Dimetrodon is technically not a dinosaur—and it's not a reptile either! It is actually considered a relative of primitive mammals that lived more than 270 million years ago.

Maiasaura

Maiasaura means "good mother reptile" for good reason! Evidence suggests that the Maiasaura chewed food for its babies while caring for them in closely guarded nests.

Fun Fact!

Size:
30 feet long

Weight:
3 tons

Diet:
Herbivore

This duck-billed dinosaur had a long snout and a small crest above each eye. Maiasaura walked the lands of what is now Montana during the Cretaceous Period.

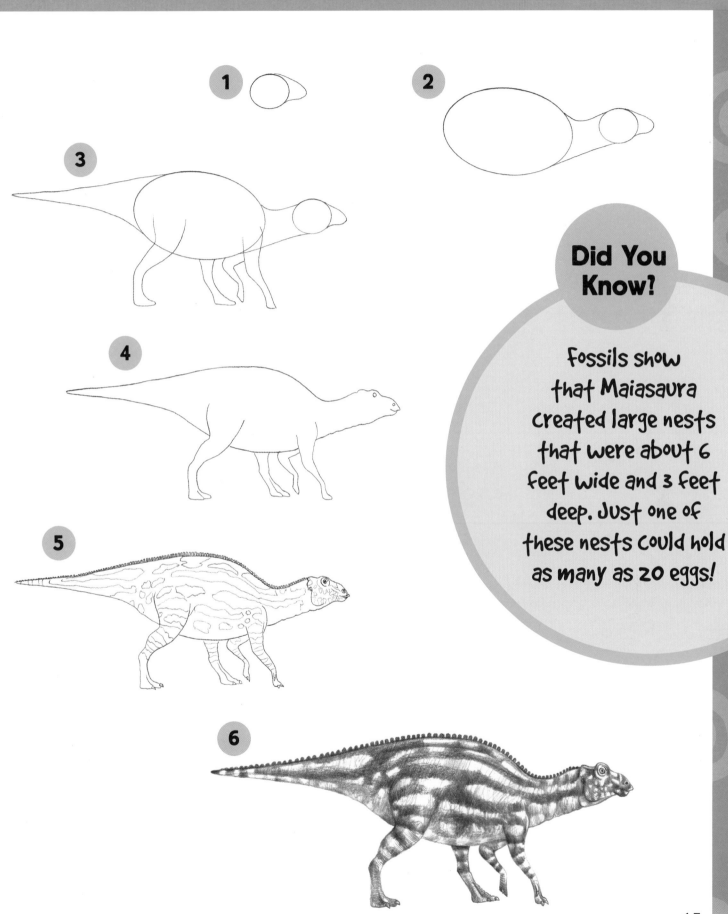

Did You Know?

fossils show that Maiasaura created large nests that were about 6 feet wide and 3 feet deep. Just one of these nests could hold as many as 20 eggs!

15

Velociraptor

Did You Know?

The Velociraptor shared several characteristics with modern birds, such as feathers, hollow bones, and nesting instincts.

Diet:
Carnivore

Weight:
100 pounds

Size:
6 feet long

Velociraptor was a small, smart, and speedy predator that existed during the Late Cretaceous Period on the Asian continent.

Fun Fact!

Watch out for those feet! The Velociraptor is known for its retractable, sickle-shaped claw on the second toe of each foot. This useful feature helped capture prey.

Stegosaurus

Fun Fact!

The Stegosaurus is not known for its intelligence. Although the dinosaur's body is often compared to the size of a bus, its brain was about the size of a walnut.

Size:
30 feet long

Weight:
3 tons

Diet:
Herbivore

Discovered in the North American West, this Late Jurassic dinosaur had a small head, a spiky tail, and two rows of large, bony plates that stood up along its spine.

Mini Quiz

True or false? Stegosaurus plates acted as a defense against predators.

(Answer on page 64)

Brachiosaurus

Did You Know?

The Brachiosaurus was among the heaviest dinosaurs of all time. Some scientists estimate its weight at 88 tons, which is more than 176,000 pounds! Its estimated life span was 100 years.

Size:
85 feet long

Diet:
Herbivore

Weight:
50 tons

Brachiosaurus was an enormous dinosaur with tall front legs and a very long neck, which enabled it to eat leaves high up in the trees.

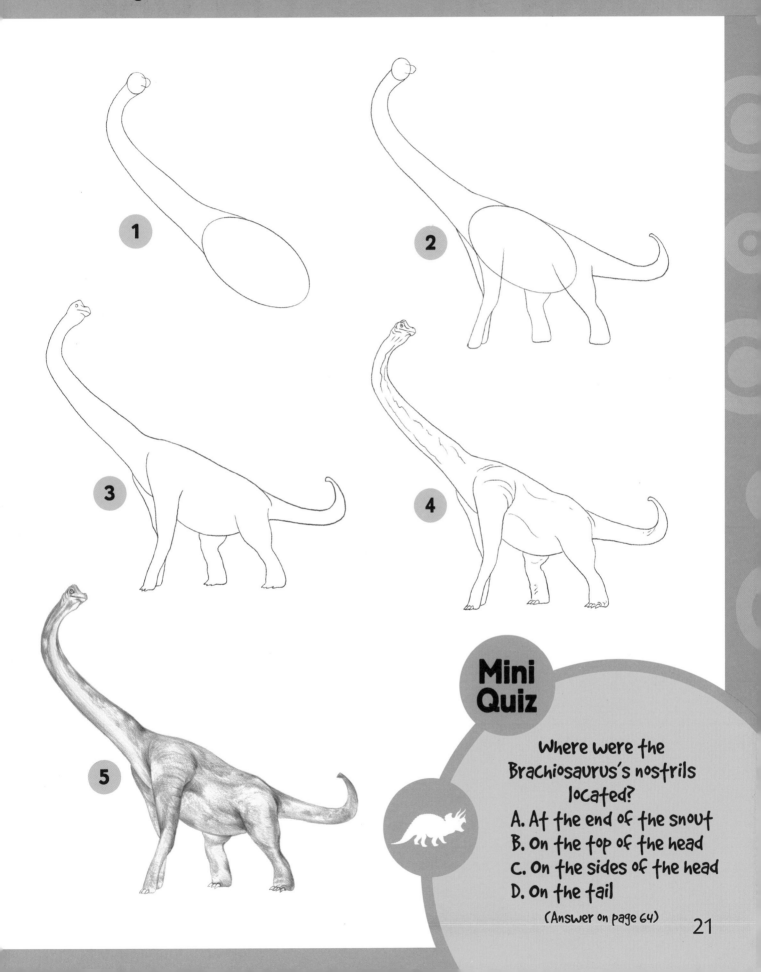

Mini Quiz

Where were the Brachiosaurus's nostrils located?
A. At the end of the snout
B. On the top of the head
C. On the sides of the head
D. On the tail

(Answer on page 64)

Allosaurus

Weight:
2 tons

Diet:
Carnivore

Size:
35 feet long

Fun Fact!

Unlike fellow carnivores Albertosaurus and Tyrannosaurus rex, which had two forelimb fingers, Allosaurus had three fingers with sharp claws.

This bipedal beast from the Late Jurassic Period had a strong, massive tail and a large skull with rough ridges near the eyes.

1

2

3

4

5

6

Mini Quiz

Allosaurus serves as the state fossil for which of the following states:
A. Texas
B. Alaska
C. Utah
D. Florida

(Answer on page 64)

Mamenchisaurus

The Mamenchisaurus had one of the longest necks of any dinosaur on earth. With 19 giant but lightweight vertebrae, its neck was roughly 36 feet long—about the length of the rest of its body (tail included!).

Fun Fact!

Diet:
Herbivore

Weight:
40 tons

Size:
70 feet long

Mamenchisaurus roamed the lands of Asia during the Late Jurassic Period. This long-necked herbivore could reach both low and very high vegetation.

Unlike most plant eaters today, the teeth of the Mamenchisaurus were not used to grind plant matter. Instead, they were used to strip off leaves, which the dinosaur then swallowed whole.

Did You Know?

Compsognathus

Diet:
Carnivore

Weight:
12 pounds

Size:
3 feet long

Fun Fact!

Scientists uncovered two nearly complete fossilized skeletons of Compsognathus in France and Germany. Scientists also found the remains of lizards in their bellies, giving clues about this dinosaur's carnivorous diet.

Compsognathus was quick and slender, with a long neck and tail. This tiny dinosaur roamed Europe during the Late Jurassic Period.

Mini Quiz

Scientists often compare the size of Compsognathus to the following:
A. A rat
B. A chicken
C. A fox
D. A wolf

(Answer on page 64)

Iguanodon

Iguanodon refers to the dinosaur's teeth, which resembled those of today's iguana. The Iguanodon also had jointed jaws and back teeth with a sloping surface that enabled it to chew hard plant material.

Fun Fact!

Weight:
3 tons

Diet:
Herbivore

Size:
30 feet long

This heavy herbivore grazed the earth during the Cretaceous Period. It is known for its complex forelimbs and its ability to walk on two or four legs.

Did You Know?

The Iguanodon's forelimbs were very complex. Each five-fingered hand had a large spike for a thumb and a *prehensile* (or grasping) "pinkie" finger.

Quetzalcoatlus

Diet:
Carnivore

Weight:
Up to 500 pounds

Size:
36-foot wingspan

Fun Fact!

Both pterosaurs and dinosaurs are more closely related to birds than other dinosaur-like reptiles today, including crocodiles!

This flying prehistoric reptile had a sharp beak and long neck. Its wings were made of stretched leathery skin and spanned nearly 40 feet from tip to tip!

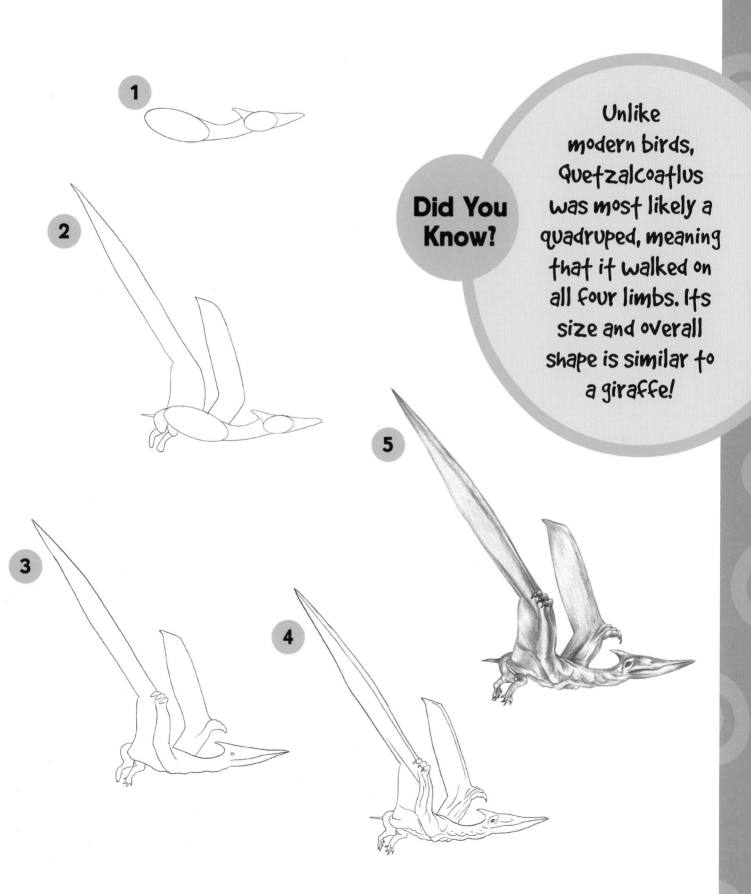

Did You Know?

Unlike modern birds, Quetzalcoatlus was most likely a quadruped, meaning that it walked on all four limbs. Its size and overall shape is similar to a giraffe!

Styracosaurus

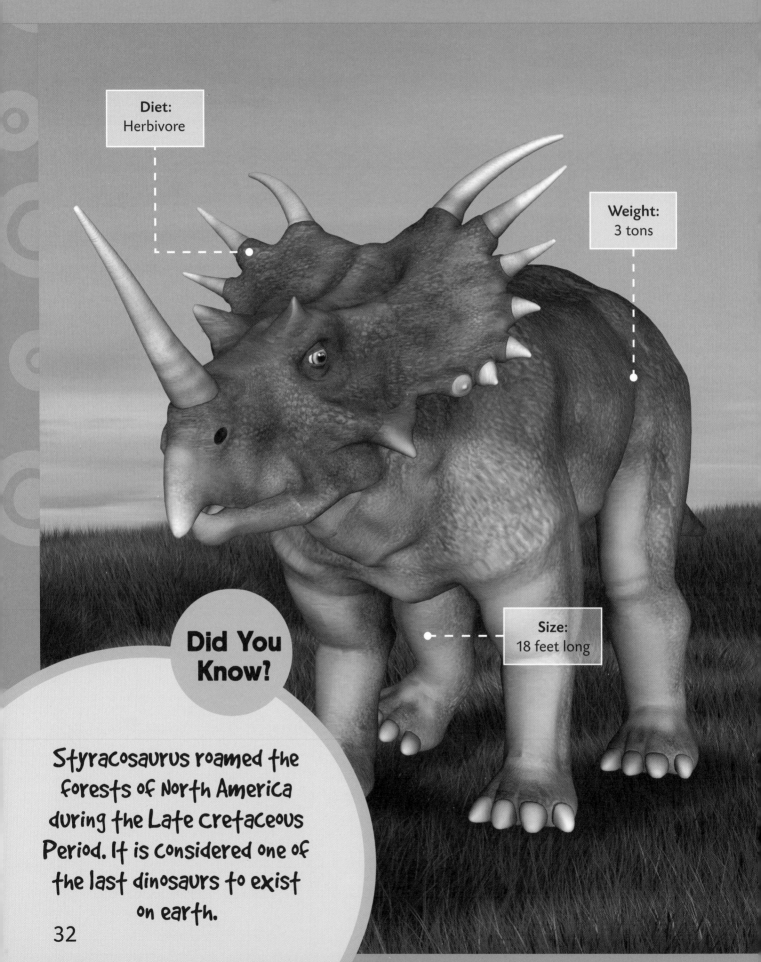

Diet:
Herbivore

Weight:
3 tons

Size:
18 feet long

Did You Know?

Styracosaurus roamed the forests of North America during the Late Cretaceous Period. It is considered one of the last dinosaurs to exist on earth.

A smaller relative of the Triceratops, this intimidating herbivore had a prominent nasal horn and a spiky frill of bone behind its head.

Mini Quiz

What does the name *Styracosaurus* mean in Ancient Greek?
A. Spiked lizard
B. Horned lizard
C. Nose lizard
D. Deadly lizard
(Answer on page 64)

Parasaurolophus

Parasaurolophus was mainly a quadruped, but scientists believe it could also rear up and possibly run on its hind legs. This gave the dinosaur access to a range of plant heights while eating.

Did You Know?

Weight:
3 tons

Diet:
Herbivore

Size:
33 feet long

Parasaurolophus roamed North America during the Cretaceous Period. This duck-billed herbivore had a distinct head crest that curved up and over the skull.

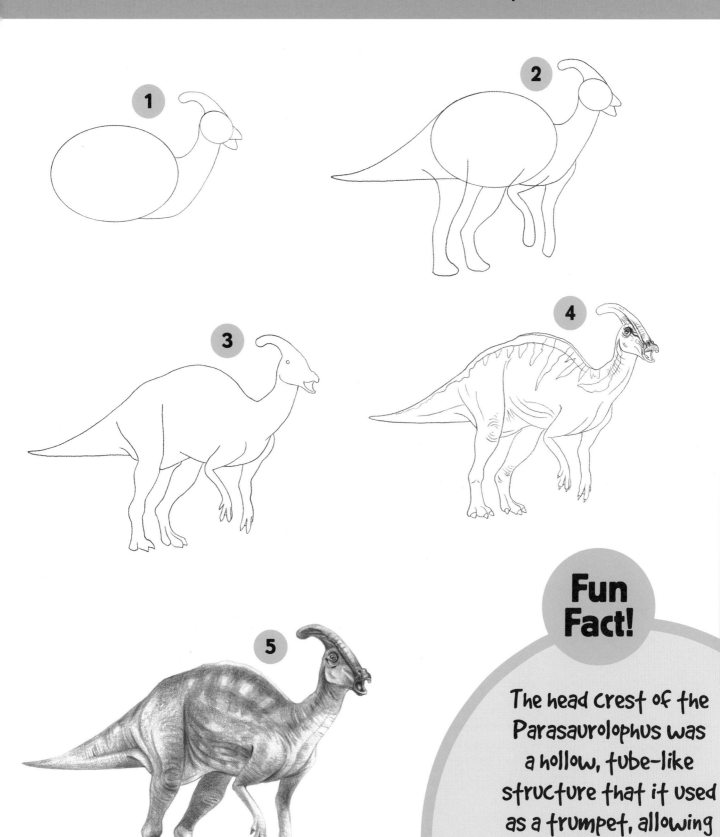

Fun Fact!

The head crest of the Parasaurolophus was a hollow, tube-like structure that it used as a trumpet, allowing it to communicate with others in its herd.

Baryonyx

Did You Know?

The name of this fish-eating dinosaur means "heavy claw." Scientists suspect that it used its abnormally large thumb claw to catch fish in the water!

Weight: 2 tons

Diet: Carnivore

Size: 28 feet long

Baryonyx had large claws and a flat, crocodile-like head with a mouth full of teeth. It roamed the lands of Europe and Africa during the Cretaceous Period.

Fun Fact!

In 1983, a fossil hunter discovered a Baryonyx near Dorking, England, making it the first carnivorous dinosaur unearthed in Britain!

Kentrosaurus

Did You Know?

Despite a stiff, spiky appearance, the Kentrosaurus was a rather agile beast. It had a flexible neck and hips and could swing its spiky tail 180 degrees. Scientists believe that it could also rear up on its hind legs to access food.

Weight:
2 tons

Size:
15 feet long

Diet:
Herbivore

Kentrosaurus was a well-armed herbivore with a small head, beaked mouth, and two rows of bony plates and spikes adorning its back.

Fun Fact!

About half the size of its Stegosaurus cousin, this Late Jurassic beast stood about 6 feet tall—about the height of a man.

Utahraptor

Utahraptor was discovered in 1991 by a trio of paleontologists in Moab, Utah. What they believed to be a rib of a different type of dinosaur turned out to be the claw of this large raptor.

Did You Know?

Diet:
Carnivore

Weight:
1 ton

Size:
20 feet long

This intelligent predator had strong hind legs and long, sharp claws. One claw on each limb was noticeably larger than the others, reaching up to 8 inches in length!

Mini Quiz

What does the suffix "-raptor" mean in Latin?
A. Thief
B. Killer
C. Leader
D. Runner
(Answer on page 64)

Triceratops

As one of the largest land mammals ever to roam the earth, the skull of the Triceratops was 10 feet long and 7 feet wide!

Fun Fact!

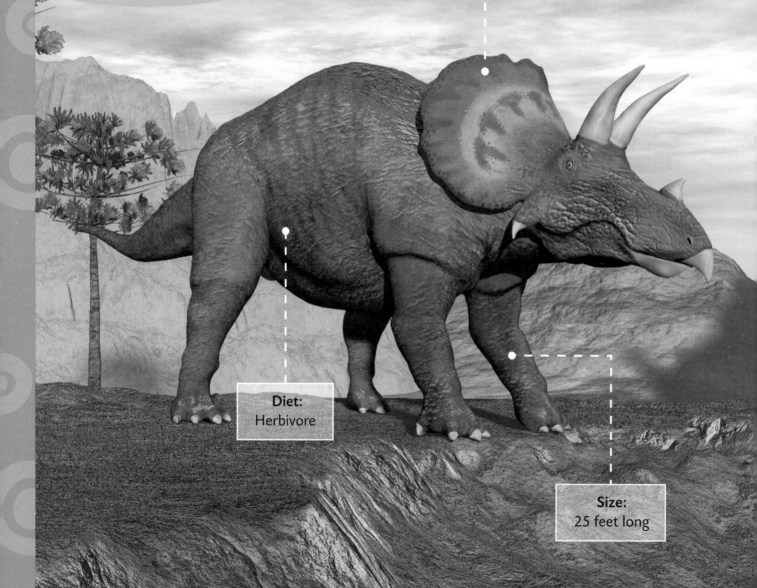

Weight:
10 tons

Diet:
Herbivore

Size:
25 feet long

With a name meaning "three-horned face," this herbivore had a giant skull with three sharp horns and a bony frill at the back of the head.

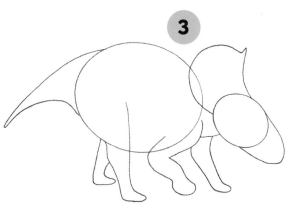

Did You Know? Scientists believe that most of the head was covered in keratin—a fibrous protein that makes up hair, nails, feathers, and horns. Because keratin is sometimes colorful in nature, it's possible that the Triceratops was a very colorful creature!

Pachycephalosaurus

Weight:
1,000 pounds

Size:
15 feet

Diet:
Herbivore

Fun Fact!

Scientists believe that the Pachycephalosaurus used its thick, weapon-like skull to head-butt rivals in a show of dominance. It may have also head-butted predators in self-defense.

Named "thick-headed lizard," Pachycephalosaurus was a bipedal herbivore with keen eyesight and a thick, dome-shaped skull surrounded by spikes and knobs.

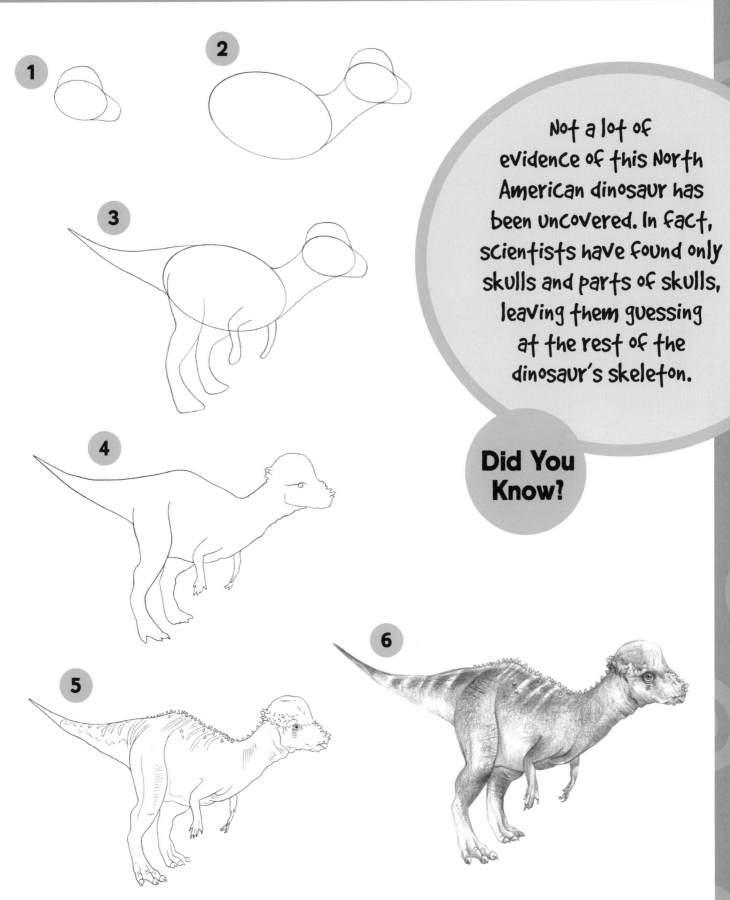

Not a lot of evidence of this North American dinosaur has been uncovered. In fact, scientists have found only skulls and parts of skulls, leaving them guessing at the rest of the dinosaur's skeleton.

Did You Know?

Tyrannosaurus Rex

Weight:
9 tons

Diet:
Carnivore

Size:
40 feet long

Did You Know?

T. rex had giant, serrated teeth that were larger than any other dinosaur's. one discovered tooth was a foot in length!

Called "T. rex" for short, this terrifying and legendary dinosaur had a large head, powerful jaws, strong forelegs, and small arms.

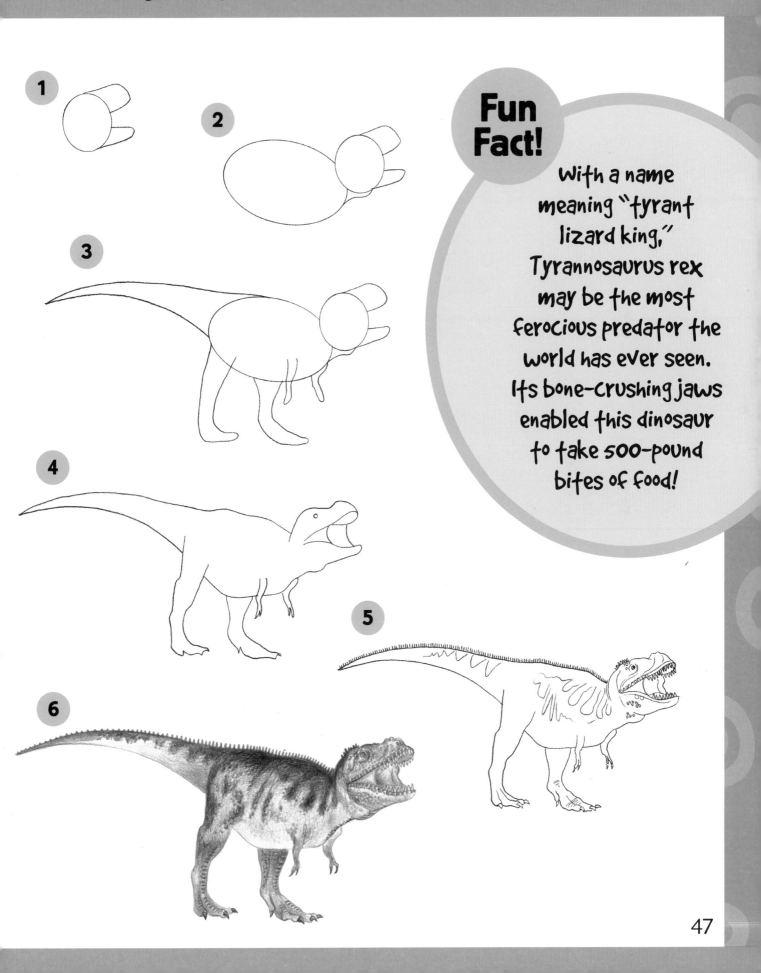

Fun Fact!

With a name meaning "tyrant lizard king," Tyrannosaurus rex may be the most ferocious predator the world has ever seen. Its bone-crushing jaws enabled this dinosaur to take 500-pound bites of food!

Polacanthus

Diet:
Herbivore

Weight:
5 tons

Size:
15 feet long

Fun Fact!

The word *Polacanthus* comes from the Ancient Greek words for "many thorns," describing the dinosaur's striking features.

This dinosaur of the early Cretaceous Period was unearthed in England. Resembling Ankylosaurus, Polacanthus was well protected with a coat of bony armor.

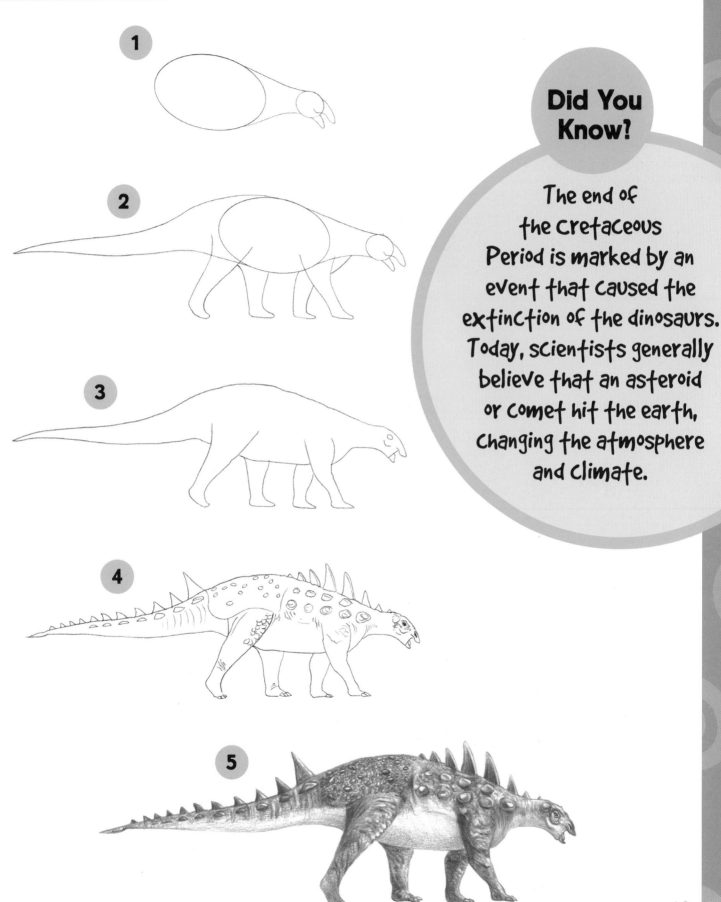

Did You Know?

The end of the Cretaceous Period is marked by an event that caused the extinction of the dinosaurs. Today, scientists generally believe that an asteroid or comet hit the earth, changing the atmosphere and climate.

49

Ornithomimus

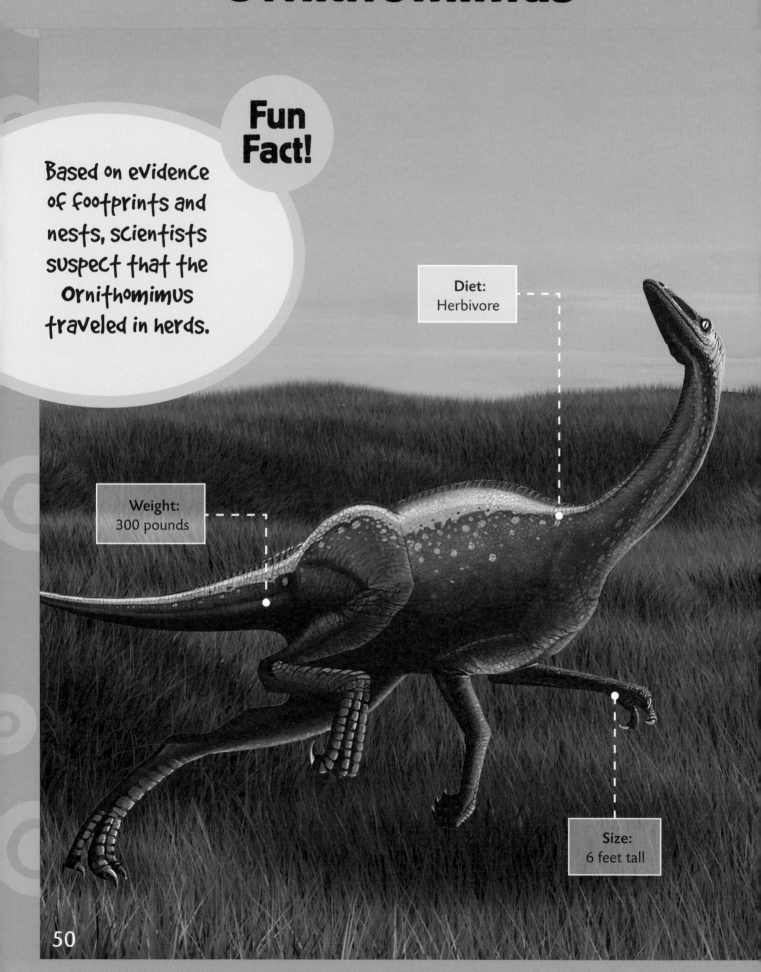

Fun Fact!

Based on evidence of footprints and nests, scientists suspect that the Ornithomimus traveled in herds.

Diet:
Herbivore

Weight:
300 pounds

Size:
6 feet tall

This ostrich-like dinosaur had a long neck, large eyes, and a body covered in feathers. Long, powerful legs paired with a light body made it a fast runner.

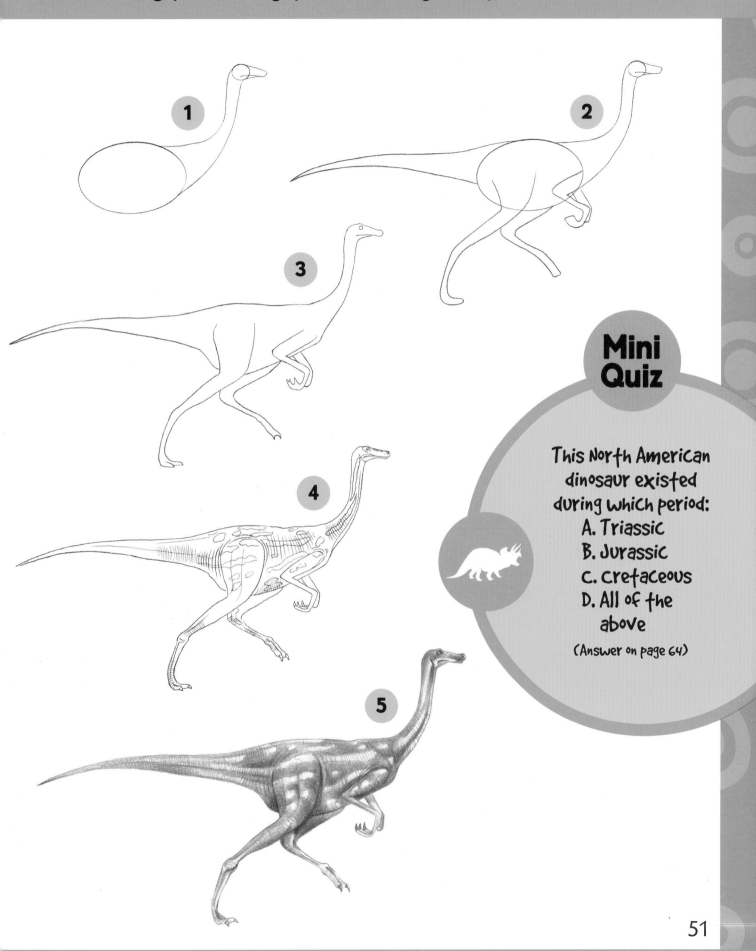

Mini Quiz

This North American dinosaur existed during which period:
A. Triassic
B. Jurassic
C. Cretaceous
D. All of the above

(Answer on page 64)

Protoceratops

Fun Fact!

Protoceratops was discovered in Mongolia. Based on fossil evidence of a fight in progress, one of its enemies was the Velociraptor.

Weight:
400 pounds

Size:
6 feet long

Diet:
Herbivore

Protoceratops was a quadrupedal herbivore with a beaked mouth, cheek teeth, and a large skull with a bony frill that grew back over its head.

Did You Know?

Lambeosaurus

Did You Know?

The function of the bony crest is unknown; however, most scientists believe it either helped produce sound or enhanced the dinosaur's sense of smell.

Size:
40 feet long

Weight:
5 tons

Diet:
Herbivore

This duck-billed dinosaur is known for the unique bony crest atop the head. Lambeosaurus roamed North America during the Cretaceous Period.

Fun Fact!

Based on skin impressions found in fossils, scientists believe that the Lambeosaurus was coated with polygonal scales.

Troodon

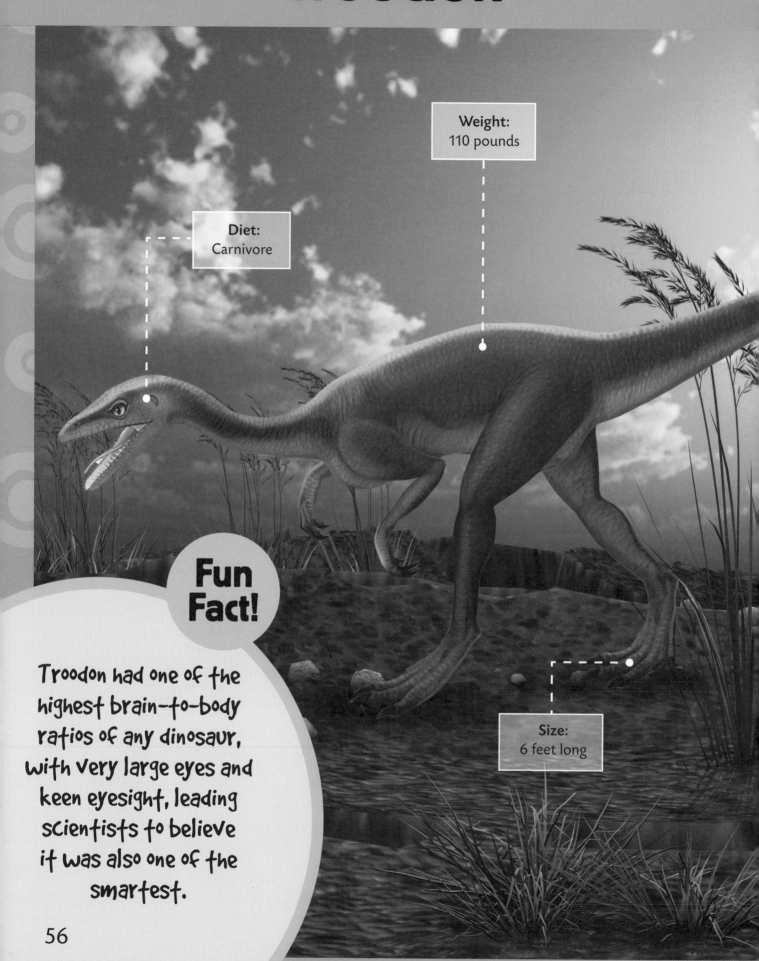

Weight:
110 pounds

Diet:
Carnivore

Size:
6 feet long

Fun Fact!

Troodon had one of the highest brain-to-body ratios of any dinosaur, with very large eyes and keen eyesight, leading scientists to believe it was also one of the smartest.

The bipedal Troodon had a large, sleek head and a stiff tail. With a lightweight body and strong hind legs, this intelligent dinosaur was built for speed.

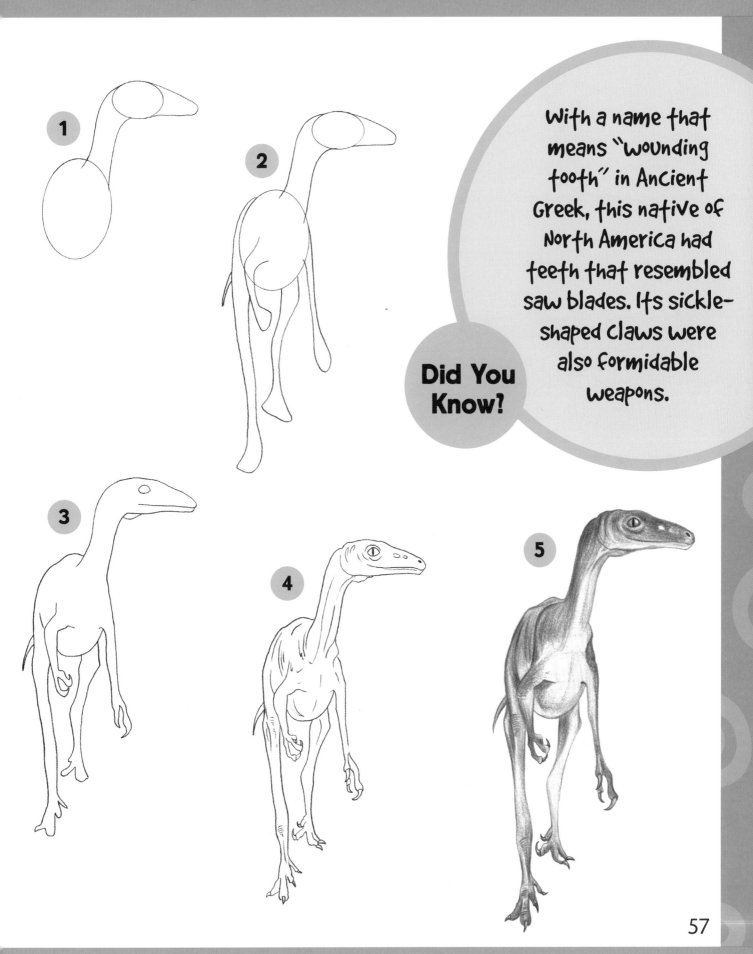

Did You Know?

With a name that means "wounding tooth" in Ancient Greek, this native of North America had teeth that resembled saw blades. Its sickle-shaped claws were also formidable weapons.

Giganotosaurus

Weight:
6 tons

Size:
40 feet long

Diet:
Carnivore

Fun Fact!

Giganotosaurus's brain-to-body ratio suggests that its intelligence was similar to that of a modern reptile.

Discovered in southern Argentina, Giganotosaurus was comparable to the mighty Tyrannosaurus rex. This bipedal carnivore thrived during the Cretaceous Period.

1

2

3

Mini Quiz

True or false? The diet of Giganotosaurus consisted of fish and lizards.

(Answer on page 64)

4

5

6

Spinosaurus

Weight:
20 tons

Diet:
Carnivore

Size:
50 feet long

Did You Know?

Spinosaurus was unearthed in North Africa, which was once covered in rivers and wetlands.

Spinosaurus was a huge carnivorous beast that lived both in water and on land during the Cretaceous Period. It had a large "sail" of skin and spines along its back.

Fun Fact!

Spinosaurus holds two important distinctions. It was the largest carnivore to ever walk the earth— even larger than the Tyrannosaurus rex! It is also considered to be the first swimming dinosaur.

Albertosaurus

Weight:
2 tons

Size:
25 feet long

Diet:
Carnivore

Fun Fact!

Albertosaurus had long, well-built rear legs that made it a quick runner. Juveniles may have reached speeds of up to 40 miles per hour!

This bipedal carnivore had a large head, small arms, and a mouth full of serrated teeth. Named after a Canadian province, evidence suggests that it may have hunted in packs.

Mini Quiz

Albertosaurus is considered a cousin to which of the following:
A. Tyrannosaurus rex
B. Stegosaurus
C. Triceratops
D. Velociraptor
(Answer on page 64)

1

2

3

4

5

Mini Quiz Answers

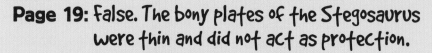

Page 19: False. The bony plates of the Stegosaurus were thin and did not act as protection.

Page 21: B. The nostrils of the Brachiosaurus were located on the top of its head.

Page 23: C. Allosaurus is the state fossil for Utah.

Page 27: B. Scientists often compare Compsognathus to a chicken or a turkey.

Page 33: A. *Styracosaurus* means "spiked lizard" in Ancient Greek.

Page 41: A. The suffix "-raptor" means "thief" or "robber" in Latin.

Page 51: C. Ornithomimus existed during the Late Cretaceous Period.

Page 59: False. Giganotosaurus hunted and ate large, plant-eating dinosaurs.

Page 63: A. Albertosaurus is considered a cousin to the Tyrannosaurus rex.